50 THRIFTY DIY
LAMPSHADES

D&C
David and Charles

Contents

Making a lampshade

Making lampshades using self-adhesive backing material is a simple technique that anyone can master.

Materials required

- lampshade ring sets or

- plain rings or

- tapered lampshade rings

- clips to clip onto bulbs, pyramid frames, wall-mounted frames or any other frame, depending on the desired shape

- white or transparent self-adhesive backing material

- thick vinyl glue or PVA glue

- strong double-sided sticky tape to stick the lampshade together

- self-adhesive binding tape

- and, of course, all kinds of fabric, paper, braids, etc. Let your imagination run wild!

Tools required

You will not need to spend very much:

- pair of dressmaking scissors and pair of paper scissors

- cutter

- metal ruler

- cutting mat

- hole punch

- pair of pliers

- small paintbrush cut to a point for the glue

- wooden clothes pegs

Frames

Lampshades are made with rings, frameworks or other oval, square or rectangular shapes, as well as copper structures coated with white epoxy paint.

A traditional conical, drum or cylindrical shade is made with two separate rings that are stuck to self-adhesive backing material.

The lampshade must always have a wide opening to enable the heat of the bulb to dissipate.

For a table lamp, the lampshade ring set is at the base of the lampshade and the plain ring is at the top. These rings are inverted if you want to make a pendant light. A lampshade ring set is a plain ring with the mounting ring for the lamp holder at its centre.

To make a pyramid or wall-mounted lampshade, a framework is used onto which the self-adhesive backing material is stuck, covered with the desired material.

Ring sets for tapered shades are used for scalloped lampshades or other decorative edgings. These lampshades are stuck together at the top, but the bottom of the lampshade is cut in a decorative way: there is therefore no ring at the bottom.

Clips that clip onto the bulbs are also available and are used to make small shades for a chandelier.

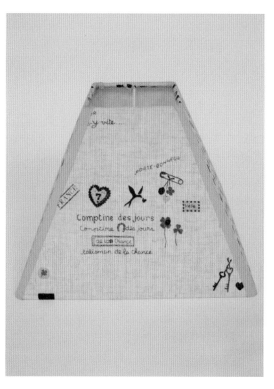

5

Introduction

Self-adhesive backing material

Self-adhesive backing material diffuses the light and gives the required rigidity to the lampshade.

The front is white or transparent; the reverse is a film grid that is carefully removed, so that paper or fabric can be stuck to it.

The white self-adhesive backing material is the most traditional and the most commonly used. The transparent self-adhesive backing material is suitable for certain decorative papers so as to reveal their luminosity. It also enables the inside of a fabric to be highlighted, if you so wish. Self-adhesive backing material is bought by the metre; it is available in a width of 1.2m (1.2yd).

Covering the self-adhesive backing material

Any type of fabric may be stuck to the self-adhesive backing material, but it is best to avoid synthetic fabrics and go for natural ones instead, e.g. linen, cotton, silk, etc.

Wrapping paper, fibre paper or wallpaper can also be applied to the self-adhesive backing material. This is not an exhaustive list.

If you would like a strong light, then it is better to choose a fine, clear fabric. However, for a decorative lampshade (often used for accent lighting around the home) you can have fun choosing more original materials and colours.

Glue the covered self-adhesive backing material onto the rings or the framework with some vinyl glue, i.e. a thick PVA glue that you apply between the self-adhesive backing material and the metal with a paintbrush.

Leave it to dry for about an hour, held together with several clothes pegs.

Stick the lampshade together with some strong double-sided sticky tape.

Pattern

To make a lampshade you need a pattern. For a damaged lampshade that you would like to revamp, carefully remove the old cover and trace it onto the self-adhesive backing material using a pencil, to make an identical lampshade using the original rings.

To make a new lampshade, design the template:

- *For a cylindrical lampshade*, two rings with the same diameter, this is easy: multiply the diameter of the lampshade by 3.14 to obtain its circumference and add 1.5cm (⅝in) for sticking the lampshade together.

This will make a rectangle, with the height being that of the height of the lampshade.

- *For a conical lampshade*, where the two diameters are different, the template has to be a geometric construction that needs to be calculated. In shops that sell lampshade accessories, you can also find template boards and sewing patterns, which means you can avoid having to make this calculation!

- *For a pyramid lampshade* or a wall-mounted shade, place the frame against the self-adhesive backing material to draw the template that corresponds to the framework.

- *Upcycling idea!* Old lampshades found in second-hand shops or car boot sales can be used as templates once you have removed their coverings.

Finishes

You can apply a self-adhesive binding tape to finish off the edge of the lampshade.

Alternatively, you can leave an overlap of 1cm (⅜in) of fabric and turn it up inside the lampshade.

You can glue on braids too:

The main braid used is military braid: a little cord approximately 3mm (⅛in) wide that enhances the lampshade. They come in all sorts of colours and finishes: serge, grosgrain, serpentine, etc. – the choice is vast. You can finish a lampshade with a coat of varnish. This is a simple finish that is ideal for the beginner. Make little holes with a hole punch every 2cm (¾in) on the covered self-adhesive backing before the lampshade is assembled. The ribbon keeps the rings attached to the cover, so there is no need for glue.

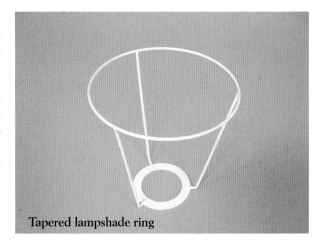

Tapered lampshade ring

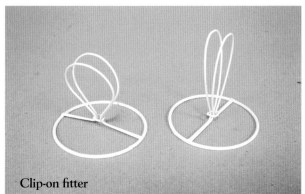

Clip-on fitter

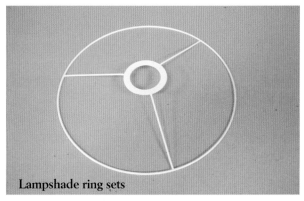

Lampshade ring sets

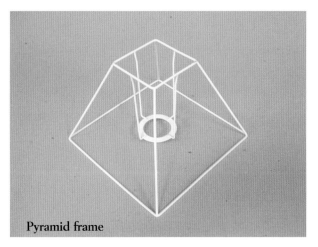

Pyramid frame

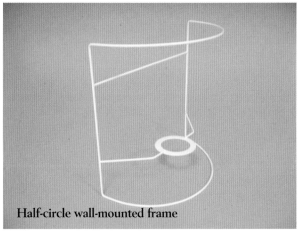

Half-circle wall-mounted frame

Making a cylindrical lampshade from wallpaper

The cylindrical lampshade is a very easy lampshade to make and is ideal for beginners.

You need to use two rings of the same diameter: a lampshade ring set (ring with a smaller ring), onto which the lamp holder will be screwed, and a plain ring.

Cylindrical lampshades can be placed on a lampstand.

The lampshade ring set will be at the bottom. If you want to make a pendant, the lampshade ring set will then be at the top, so that you can hang the lampshade from the ceiling (see Fig. 1).

The lampshade made here is 30cm (12in) in diameter. The rings used are therefore a lampshade ring set 30cm (12in) in diameter and a plain ring 30cm (12in) in diameter.

The height is 20cm (8in).

Prepare a rectangle of self-adhesive backing material, 95.7cm (27¾in) long (30cm (12in) × 3.14 + 1.5cm (⅝in) for sticking the lampshade together) with a height of 20cm (8in) (see Fig. 2).

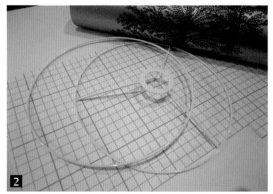

Wallpapers are very useful these days for decorating rooms; an offcut will enable you to make very effective lampshades!

As the wallpaper is 55cm (22in) wide, you will need to make a join by slightly overlapping the two pieces of wallpaper in the centre of the shade.

Prepare the two pieces of wallpaper, approximately 22cm (8¾in) high, so that there is a little gap on each side, and 48cm (19in) long, so that the join is in the centre.

8

Place the wallpaper on the self-adhesive backing material, grid side uppermost, and apply gradually, pressing down firmly. Overlap the two pieces of self-adhesive backing material by 2mm (⅛in). Overlap the two pieces of wallpaper by 2mm (⅛in).

Once the wallpaper is stuck down, cut off all the excess paper that overlaps the self-adhesive backing material.

Place a strip of strong, double-sided sticky tape 1.2cm (½in) wide onto the inside edge of the lampshade, peel back the protective film and stick the lampshade together.

Place one of the two rings against the edge of the lampshade using clothes pegs and start to glue. Use thick vinyl glue.

Apply the glue generously with a paintbrush between the cover and the ring.

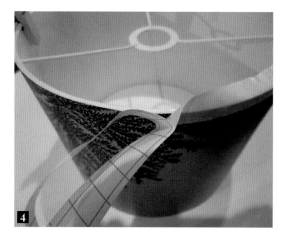

Wait approximately one hour for the glue to take, remove the clothes pegs and proceed in the same way with the second ring (see Fig. 3).

Once the lampshade is well stuck down, proceed with the decorative finishes using a self-adhesive binding tape (see Fig. 4).

One third of the edging is visible on the lampshade and the remaining two thirds are wrapped around the ring towards the inside of the shade (see Fig. 5).

After applying the self-adhesive binding tape around the lampshade, place a grosgrain decorative braid along the edge of the shade using vinyl glue to stick it down (see Fig. 6).

Making a conical lampshade – a portable lamp in fabric

Portable lamps are little lampshades that are wired up to the electricity supply that can be hung up or moved around as you wish. These lights are great for small spaces, such as the understairs cupboard, children's rooms, etc. The fabric chosen is lightweight cotton, which allows the light to filter through nicely (see Fig. 1).

Cut out the white self-adhesive backing material according to the shape of the portable lamp (see Fig. 2), with a diameter of 15cm (6in) at the bottom and 8cm (7¼in) at the top. The slope is 19cm (7½in). Calculate the template or transfer onto template paper that you have purchased.

AB = radius, large ring of the shade
AC = height of the shade
CD = radius, small ring of the shade
Trace a straight line passing through B and D, to find O, the centre of the curves passing through A and C.
Calculate the angle for the opening:
$\{(AB - CD) \times 360\}/AC$.
Transfer this angle onto **O**.

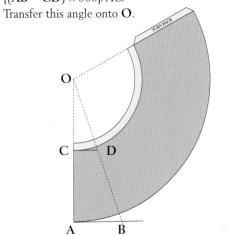

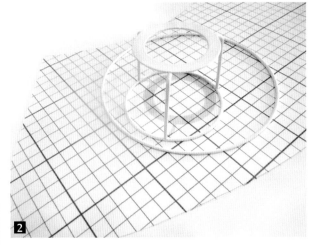

10

You will need a ring 8cm (3¼in) in diameter with a 5cm (2in) smaller ring for the top, at the point where the electrical fixtures will be integrated, and a 15cm (6in) ring for the bottom. Cut out a rectangle of fabric a little larger than the shape cut from self-adhesive backing material and iron it carefully so that there are no creases.

Place the fabric on the self-adhesive backing material, grid side uppermost (see Fig. 3).

Glue the fabric by gradually removing the protective film of the self-adhesive backing material and smoothing the material with the palm of your hand towards the top and bottom to remove any air bubbles.

Cut off the excess fabric all around the self-adhesive backing material, leaving 1cm (⅜in) of fabric along one of the vertical seams (see Fig. 4). Turn this under to the inside of the self-adhesive backing material after applying the vinyl glue. This will give a very neat seam.

Place some strong double-sided sticky tape onto the fabric turn-back, so that you can stick the lampshade together. Stick the lampshade together.

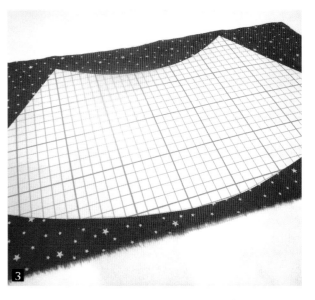

Making a conical lampshade – a portable lamp in fabric (cont.)

Line up the 15cm (6in) ring, holding it in place with wooden clothes pegs, and apply vinyl glue with a paintbrush between the ring and the self-adhesive backing material (see Fig. 5). Distribute the clothes pegs equally (see Fig. 6). Leave to dry for a good hour and repeat with the second ring.

Once the rings are stuck down well, if the self-adhesive backing material overlaps the rings a little, cut off the excess using scissors (see Fig. 7).

For this portable lamp, a self-adhesive binding tape in the same fabric has been made by sticking 1.5cm (⅝in) of flexible, double-sided sticky tape onto the fabric. You can also use a ready-made, coloured self-adhesive binding tape.

5

6

Place the self-adhesive binding tape onto the largest ring, starting at the seam of the shade (see Fig. 8).

One third of the edging must be on the cover and the remaining two thirds will be wrapped around the ring towards the inside of the lampshade.

Press down well with your fingernail to push the edging towards the inside of the ring. Repeat with the small ring.

Always work with the electricity switched off.

To connect to the electricity supply, thread the cable holder onto the cable, then mount the lamp holder by screwing it to the cable holder.

Make a little loop in the electricity cable with a ribbon that matches the fabric to hang the portable lamp wherever you like around your home!

You can buy an electric light fitting from a DIY store with all the required parts: bulb, lamp holder, attachment ring, cable, switch and plug.

Wool and fabric

Patchwork lamp

Materials

• Lampstand • Spray paint • Transparent varnish • Straight-sided lampshade frame • Self-adhesive backing material • Selection of silk scarves • Braids • Vinyl glue • Adhesive percale ribbon • Double-sided sticky tape

Instructions

Wash, then iron the silk scarves.

Cut a piece of self-adhesive backing material long enough to cover the outside of the lampshade + 2cm (¾in) × the exact height of the shade.

Cut strips of scarf and apply them side by side onto the self-adhesive backing material, gradually pulling back the plastic film and ensuring that there are no bubbles.

Leave the width of the overlap, at one end, without any fabric. Glue braids using fabric glue along the joins of the scarves.

Close up the self-adhesive backing material to form a circle with some double-sided sticky tape.

Glue the self-adhesive backing material onto the top of the framework using vinyl glue.

Leave to dry, holding in place with clothes pegs. Glue the bottom in the same way.

Attach adhesive percale ribbon across the join on the lampshade for a professional finish.

Fringed lampshade

Materials

• Framework: 1 piece of red taffeta: for the width measurements take the widest part of the lampshade + 2cm (¾in) for the seams; height: height of the lampshade + 3cm (1¼in) at the top and + 20cm (8in) at the bottom
• Matching thread • Fine decorative cord
• Beads

Instructions

Close up the taffeta into a circle. Iron the seam flat.

Fringe the top and bottom of the 'skirt'.

Pull the threads. The taffeta will gather very easily. Hold the fringes in place with some little stitches flush with the fabric.

Slide the skirt onto the framework. Pleat the top of the skirt to adjust it to the diameter of the top ring.

Sew the skirt onto the framework using little stitches to hold it in place.

Wind fine cord around the skirt, holding the ribbon in place with several invisible stitches.

Slip beads onto the bottom fringe, tying a knot just beneath them to hold them in place.

Wool and fabric

Traditional style

Materials

• Pendant lampshade frame with 6 panels, in empire design, approximately 40cm (16in) high • Decorative pompom ribbon, 1.5m (1.5yd) • Pencil case • Sewing box

Instructions

The shade is covered with six different fabrics sewn together.

Trace the pattern of one of the panels onto paper. Place the pattern onto the fabric. Cut all around the fabric, 1cm (⅜in) away from the pattern.

Machine sew the six pieces end to end into a long strip.

Place the strip onto the lampshade. Close up around the lampshade matching up the two ends. Tack (baste) then sew with small, invisible stitches.

Turn under the top of the bell-shaped fabric over the top ring of the framework.

Turn under at the bottom and sew by hand.

Hide the seam by sticking on a decorative pompom ribbon.

Retro lamp

Materials

• Recycled floor lamp, in wood • 2 lampshade rings identical to the originals • Natural linen • Self-adhesive backing material • 500ml (18 fl oz) of clay-based paint (white) and lime wash (clay) paint • Sandpaper • Pencil • Scissors • Double-sided sticky tape • Mini roller • Flat paintbrush • Special PVC glue • Vinyl glue • Wooden clothes pegs • Pencil case

Instructions

Dismantle the lamp. Sand the base, wash down and apply two coats of lime wash paint with a paintbrush, allowing drying time between the two coats.

Remove the cover from the lampshade as carefully as possible, so that you can save the fabric or paper and use it as a template for cutting out a piece of self-adhesive backing material.

Roughly paint a piece of linen the same size as the template in white, clay-based paint with the little roller, allowing extra paint for the flowers. Leave to dry.

Glue the self-adhesive backing material to the reverse of the painted linen. Cut out the linen, leaving a 1cm (⅜in) gap all around. Close up the self-adhesive backing material into a cylinder. Hold in place with a strip of double-sided sticky tape.

Turn under the fabric over the framework at the top and the bottom, glue and hold in place with clothes pegs whilst it dries.

Enlarge the pattern for the flowers to the size of the lampshade. Cut out and use as a template for cutting out flowers from the offcuts of painted linen.

Each flower is made of two parts of slightly different sizes, glued to one another. Fold the petals along the centre line to give them volume. Curl the edges of the petals using the blade of a pair of scissors and fray them a little.

Apply some glue to the centre of the flowers and place them on the lampshade.

Enlarge by 200%

Liberty print

Materials

• Spray paint • Self-adhesive backing material • Special high temperature glue
• Second-hand lamp, with lampshade framework • Liberty fabric remnants
• Ribbons • Fusible web • Decorative beads
• Pompoms • Heart-shaped beads

Instructions

Create a flat pattern of the shade on paper. Draw a pattern for the petals.

The lampshade is covered with eight rounded petals. Test the paper pattern against the lampshade frame.

Apply the Liberty fabrics to the self-adhesive backing material, gradually removing the protective film to avoid the formation of bubbles.

Smooth out with the palm of your hand. Cut out some 'petals' a little larger than the lampshade (see photo).

There must be enough petals to go around the lampshade when overlapping them slightly.

Cut out the same petals from self-adhesive backing material. Cover the framework by sticking a covered petal and an uncovered one back to back; the actual framework being between the two thicknesses. Overlap the petals for several cm whilst arranging them all the way around. Apply a little glue to the joins.

Paint the lampstand.

Glue pieces of wide ribbon or fabric back to back using fusible web. Cut out leaf shapes, glue them onto the pieces of straight ribbon, then attach to the lampstand or the lampshade.

Create a lucky charm by threading decorative beads and a large heart bead onto a string, then a little pompom trim. Hang the lucky charm at the bottom of the lampshade.

Knitted lampshade

Materials

• Round lampshade, 20cm (8in) in diameter, 14cm (5½in) high • 2 balls of knitting yarn (Bouton d'Or, Laika yarn, in Rocher) • 2 × no. 3 knitting needles 6.5mm (¼in)

Stitch used

Rice stitch: Work on an odd number of stitches, knit 1, purl 1 across the row = 18 sts across 10cm (4in), or 17 sts to make an odd number

Instructions

The cover of the lampshade is knitted by turning the knitting at each end. The calculation for the stitches gives 18 stitches, but it is easier to knit rice stitch on an odd number of stitches, i.e. here 17 sts, as the knitting is then the same on all the rows. However, the knitting must be taut on the lampshade. Cast (bind) off when the knitting goes right around the lampshade when pulled slightly.

Join the cast (bind) on row and the cast (bind) off row. Slide the cover onto the lampshade.

Hold in place with several stitches across the framework of the shade and the cover if the knitting has a tendency to slip.

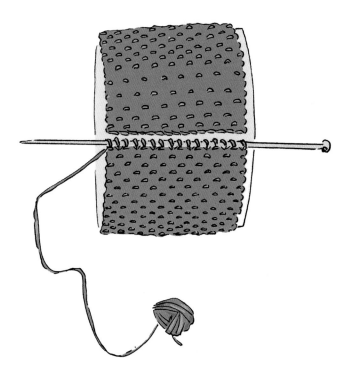

Large pendants

Materials

• Top and bottom lampshade ring,
45cm (18in) in diameter • Strip of self-adhesive
backing material, 142.5 × 53.5cm (56 × 21in)
• Double-sided sticky tape for lampshades
• Vinyl glue • Marker pen • Cutter • Ruler
• Scissors • Clothes pegs • Assortment of plain
fabrics and African motifs in strips of varying
widths, all 141.5cm (56in) in length

Instructions

Cut strips of fabric, 45cm (18in) in length (the diameter of the lampshade)
and in various widths.

Using a marker pen, draw the distribution of the strips onto the grid side of
the self-adhesive backing material.

Cut out lightly using the cutter to pierce through just the protective film.

Remove the protective strips one by one and gradually apply the fabric in
their place.

Trace a vertical line, 1cm (⅜in) from one end, on the fabric side.

Glue the self-adhesive backing material into a cylinder along this line with
some double-sided sticky tape. Leave to dry.

Glue the top and bottom rings using vinyl glue, holding them in place with
clothes pegs while they dry.

Pay attention to the direction of the lamp holder support ring: it must not
show above the edge.

Beads, ribbons and scoobies

Bohemian feel

Materials

- Metal chandelier • Turquoise spray paint
- Fuchsia paint • Bead necklace or necklace with metal rings and artificial stones in different shapes and colours • Ribbons
- Paper doilies • Candles in bright colours
- Glue • Large coloured-crystal drop beads

Instructions

Lightly sand the framework using sandpaper. Paint it with the spray paint and leave to dry.

Paint the paper doilies with the fuchsia paint, cut them in half and glue each half onto the base of each candleholder.

Assemble the artificial stones into a long necklace, spacing them with little metal rings.

Wind the necklace around the framework of the chandelier. Add the large, coloured-crystal drop beads.

Cut the ribbons to a length of approximately 40cm (16in). Slide on one or two beads per ribbon. Tie the ends of the ribbons to hold the beads in place.

Hang the ribbons, leaving the ends loose and ensuring that they are far enough away from the flames of the candles.

Slip the candles into the candle holders.

Woven ribbons

Materials

- Lampshade frame, height 20cm (8in), diameter 20cm (8in) • 1 rectangle of self-adhesive backing material, 20 × 70cm (8 × 28in) • Assortment of satin ribbons, 1cm (⅜in) wide • 2m (2yd) of braid, 2cm (¾in) wide • Vinyl glue • Pins • Cardboard • Double-sided sticky tape

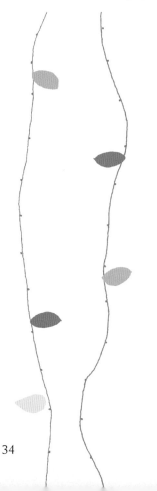

Instructions

Set up a weaving loom on the cardboard.

Lay out 22 ribbons, 1cm (⅜in) wide by 70cm (28in) long. Hold the ribbons in place at each end using pins.

Weave the weft with coloured ribbons, 22cm (8¾in) long. Vary the colours of the ribbons. Hold the ends in place using pins to uniformly stretch out the ribbons.

Cut a rectangle of self-adhesive backing material measuring 20 × 70cm (8 × 28in). Remove the plastic film and glue the self-adhesive backing material onto the weaving.

Close up the self-adhesive backing material into a cylinder against the lampshade frame, overlapping the two small sides. Hold in place with some double-sided sticky tape.

Turn under the excess strips to the inside of the shade. Glue with vinyl glue. Hold in place with clothes pegs and leave to dry.

Hide the turn-backs by sticking a 2cm (¾in) wide braid at the top and bottom of the inside of the shade

Beads, ribbons and scoobies

Beads of light

Materials

For the conical lampshade: • Translucent beads, 3mm in diameter • Galvanised frame wire, 0.4mm • Galvanised 1mm cable • Lamp holder for screw bulb with ring • Drill and fine 1mm bit • Nails

For the flat lampshade: • Translucent beads, 7mm in diameter • Galvanised frame wire, 0.7mm • Galvanised cable, 1mm • Lamp holder for screw bulb with ring • Drill and fine 1mm bit

Instructions for the conical lampshade

Pierce the ring of the lamp holder with 30 holes, 1mm in diameter.

Insert 30 nails at regular intervals into a plain wooden ring, 20cm (8in) in diameter.

Slide the lamp holder onto the neck of a bottle placed in the centre of the wooden ring, then construct the body of the lampshade by passing the frame wire alternately into a hole of the lamp holder and around a nail.

Finish by wrapping the wire around itself. Hang a length of approximately 1m (1yd) from a hole in the lamp holder, slide approximately 20 beads onto the wire then turn the frame around, wrapping the wire around the wires of the frame. Add as much wire and as many beads needed to make a lampshade approximately 20cm (8in) wide.

Remove the lampshade from its support.

Instructions for the flat lampshade

Prepare the lamp holder as above, but attach it to the centre of a rigid, plain ring (a bicycle wheel without spokes, for example).

Use the 0.7mm frame wire, which will retain the shape of the lampshade better.

Hang the lamp holder from the cable attached to the ceiling, which will support the weight of the shade. The electricity cable comes down alongside the cable and is held in place approximately every 50cm (20in) by a transparent washer.

Slightly twist the wires to shape the lampshade.

Remove the lampshade from its support.

Flower lampshade

Materials

• Frame, 17cm (6¾in) high and 30cm (12in) in diameter • 24 fine pink fluorescent strands (i.e. 1 bundle of scoobies) • 24 fine gold strands and 24 fine, fuchsia strands (i.e. 1 bundle of scoobies) (3 fuchsia strands and 1 gold strand for each flower)

Instructions

Alternate 4 gold strands, 4 fuchsia strands and 4 fluorescent strands (baguette knots) around the top ring. Continue around the frame. Pull the strands tight.

Adjust the number of strands to the diameter of the desired lampshade. Continue down to the bottom, making flat knots.

Refer to the patterns for the knots (see Scoobies). Finish off the strands by tying them. Cut the knot behind.

Make 11 decorative flowers from crochet, knitting or with a loom (a little device for making flowers), a gold heart and fuchsia petals. Tie all around the lampshade.

Diamond lampshade

Materials

• Frame, 23cm (9in) high and 25cm (10in) in diameter • Red paint • 122 fine, fuchsia strands + 12 for covering them (i.e. 3 batches of scoobies)

Instructions

Paint the frame red. Leave to dry.

Assemble the strands at the top of the frame. Make baguette knots (see Scoobies).

Continue knotting, making 18 rows of flat knots. Then begin a diamond motif in baguette knots on each side.

Finish weaving the lampshade in flat knots.

Finish off by tying the strands to the bottom of the frame. Cut the scoobies neatly.

Round lampshade

Materials

• Dome lampshade frame with 8 sections, 17cm (6¾in) high and 25cm (10cm) in diameter • Approximately 100 red scoobies • Matching paint

Instructions

Paint the frame red. Leave to dry.

Attach 12 strands between each section (baguette Knots, see Scoobies). Weave to design a diamond in baguette stitch.

At the first intersection, add a strand folded in half on each side. Weave a second diamond, adding a strand on each side. Add a strand on each side to each diamond made to increase the weaving and adapt it to the shape of the frame.

Tie the strands around the bottom ring. Leave the excess hanging down; even up the edges.

The canary has flown

Materials

- Branch • 2 yellow feathers • Lamp holder
- Electricity cable • Small 15W lamp
- Thick wire • Fine wire • Yellow glass beads
- Cutting pliers • White paint

Instructions

Paint the branch white, leave to dry. Glue on the feathers.

Prepare the bottom part of the chandelier: cut 50cm (20in) of thick wire and make eight consecutive loops. Close up into a circle to obtain a ring approximately 6cm (2¼in) in diameter (see Fig. 1).

Cut three 30cm (12in) lengths of thick wire. Bend it over and overlap at the centre of the three pieces (see Fig. 2). Slide on the beads.

Bend the ends to hook them into the loops (see Fig. 3). Join the spot where the 43 wires overlap with fine wire to hold them together. Slide on a large bead and close up with a loop.

Using the finer wire, make a horizontal grid pattern by gradually threading on beads and thus holding in place those that are on the vertical wires (see Fig. 4).

Place the lamp holder and the bulb in the cage, passing it though the loop of wire, and attach the wire to the branch.

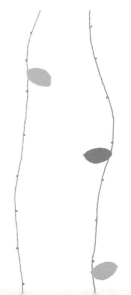

The canary has flown (cont.)

1

2

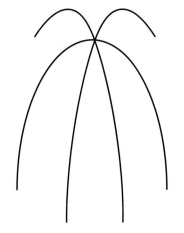

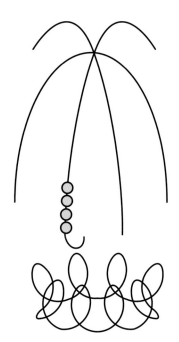

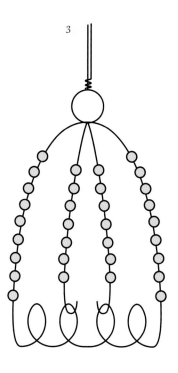

3

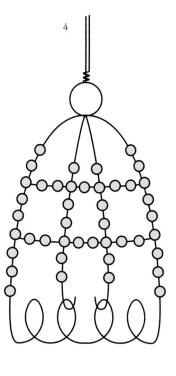

4

Spirit of the sixties

Materials

• Plank of MDF, 17 × 50cm (6¾ × 20in) × 1.6cm (⅝in) thick • 2 wooden strips, 50cm (20in) long, 1.8mm (¾in) high and 1.2cm (½in) wide • 3 flexible metal cables (with screw thread) fitted with lamp holder and electricity cable (look in the electrical department) • White acrylic paint • Olive electricity cable • Plug • 3 lampshade frames • Synthetic raffia in colours of your choice • Scoobies in matching shades • UHU super glue • Screwdriver • Drill with 9mm (⅜in) bit • Pencil • Doilies on floral printed paper • Decopatch glue varnish

Instructions

Draw a central line on the plank using a pencil. Draw three points along this line: the first at 10cm (4in), the second at 25cm (10in) and the third at 40cm (16in) along. With the 9mm (⅜in) drill, drill into each of these three points. Clean out.

Glue the wooden strips to the edges of the plank to create a raised area and leave to dry. Paint the plank white and leave to dry.

Using the Decopatch glue varnish, cover the top of the plank in paper doilies (N.B. only use the printed side).

Wrap the flexible metal cables with scoobies, gradually tying on colours of your choice. Apply a little glue here and there to hold the strands in place.

Wrap the synthetic raffia around the lampshade frames. Vary the colours. Apply a spot of glue to hold in place.

Screw the flexible metal cable into the plank. Connect the wires under the plank, then complete the electrical wiring.

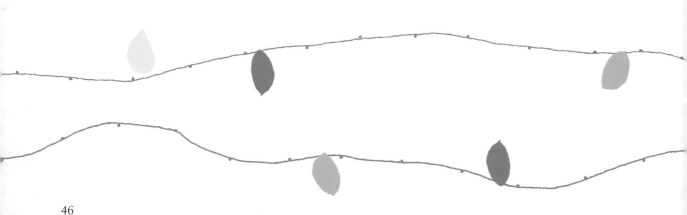

Upcycling

Fluted lampshades

Materials

• 3 fluted tart moulds, 22cm (8¾in) and 16cm (6½in) for the base, and 20cm (8in) for the lampshade • 2 threaded rods: 1 × 10cm (4in) and 1 × 2.5cm (1in) • 3 bolts, 1cm (⅜in) • 4 washers, 2.5cm (1in) with a 1cm (⅜in) central hole • Cable run connector • 2 female connectors • Bayonet lamp holder • Small bayonet lamp, 40W max. • Transparent electricity connection cable, 2m (2yd) long with switch and plug already attached • 7 or 8 small pebbles • UHU mosaic glue • Electric drill with 1cm (⅜in) bit

Instructions

Drill through the centre of the three moulds using the electric drill with the 1cm (⅜in) bit. Glue the pebbles onto the outside base of the large mould to act as weights. Leave to dry.

Place the 16cm (6½in) diameter mould onto the large mould with pebbles. Screw in the large threaded rod and hold it in place by screwing on a washer and a bolt on the outside of the two moulds. The threaded rod sticks out by 6–7cm (6½–6¾in).

At one end of the flexible metal hose screw on a female connector, followed by the cable run connector, and at the other end another female connector.

Insert the electricity cable inside the flexible hose, putting it into the hole of the cable run connector.

Unscrew the base of the lamp holder. Place a washer either side of the hole in the mould acting as the lampshade.

Screw the 2.5cm (1in)-threaded rod into the hole and into the base of the lamp holder placed inside the mould. Attach the ends of the electricity cable to the two poles of the lamp holder.

Reassemble the complete lamp holder and screw the lampshade to the flexible hose, then screw this to the lampstand.

Advice: to drill accurately in the centre of the moulds, mark the diameter line with a marker pen.

Chose pebbles that can be arranged in the mould without obstructing the hole and in such a way that the second mould can be sat evenly on top.

Use a pair of pliers to tighten the screws firmly.

Pulley lamp

Materials

- Fish-trap • Undercoat suitable for metal
- Red spray paint suitable for metal
- Foam roller • Porcelain lamp holder
- Lighting fixture • Copper-filament bulb
- Red cotton electricity cable • Rope, 4mm
(⅛in) • Pulley • Turquoise paint • Small
toolbox

Instructions

Remove the lid of the fish-trap. Paint the trap with undercoat suitable for metal using the roller. Leave to dry.

Paint with the red spray paint.

Paint the porcelain lamp holder red. Leave to dry.

Assemble the lighting fixture with the porcelain lamp holder, one copper-filament bulb and a red cotton electricity cable.

Suspend from a beam with some 4mm (⅛in) rope, passing the cable through the turquoise painted pulley.

Plastic chic

Materials

- Plastic dish or mould, e.g. jelly mould
- Lamp holder • Lighting fixture • Drill
- Small toolbox

Instruction

Pierce the top of the plastic dish. For this, you can either:

- use a cutter. This could be a little dangerous as there is a risk of cutting yourself: I would not recommend this approach.

- use a spiral drill to make a hole. Place the dish onto a workbench or a plank of wood. Spiral drills are available from DIY stores. It is always useful to have one in your toolbox.

- use a small drill. Place the dish on a stable plank of wood and hold the dish in place with some clamps. Mark the position of the hole with a permanent marker pen. Place the drill right in the centre at the top and gently drill a hole.

Whatever you do, never use the point of a pair of scissors. The hole will never be made properly and will rarely be in the right place, as the point will move out of place. Furthermore, the likelihood of having an accident is high!

Slide in the electricity cable. Attach the lamp holder inside the plastic container.

Experiment with a pretty wire and an attractive bulb.

Advice: investing in a small handheld drill can be very useful. These little tools are very practical as they are so light. You will be able to drill many small things.

Make sure that the bulb does not touch the plastic lampshade, as it could melt it.

Tin can lamp

Materials

• Tin can, 800g (1lb 12oz) • Round, transparent shade, 20cm (8in) high, to attach to lamp holder • Bolts • Washers • Lighting fixture • White lampstand • Small toolbox • Drill • White spray paint • Several pebbles • Strong glue • Double-sided sticky tape • Decorative paper • Cutter • Cutting mat • Metal ruler • Decorative sticky tape (optional)

Instructions

Open up a tin can and wash it out. Paint the can white using spray paint and leave to dry.

Drill through the top of the can with a 9mm (⅜in), heavy-duty drill bit. Slide the stand in through the hole at the top. Hold in place with the bolts and washers.

Glue several pebbles to the inside of the can to give it weight and hold the lamp.

To make the lampshade: glue strips of double-sided sticky tape, at least 20cm (8in) long, to the reverse of the paper. Using the cutter, cut the paper to the width of the sticky tape. Glue the strips of paper to the lampshade in a pleasing design, varying the directions of the strips.

Set up the lamp and assemble the whole lighting fixture.

You can also make the shade using decorative sticky tape.

Workshop chandelier

Materials

- 3 lampshade ring sets 70cm (27½in), 50cm (20in) and 30cm (12in) • Red paint
- 30 wide, flat brushes with holes in the handles •
30 flat, straight brushes with holes in the handles
- 15 round, red brushes with holes in the handles
- Lamp holder • Lighting fixture • Drill with 1cm (⅜in) wood bit

Instructions

Paint the lampshade rings and the brush handles red.

Mount the lamp holder on three lengths of cable according to the required height for hanging the chandelier, taking into consideration that the cables for the second and third rings will be longer than the height of the paintbrushes hung above.

Screw each lamp holder onto the corresponding ring and tie the cables between them to hold the rings apart. Hang the paintbrushes onto the rings. Connect to the electricity supply.

Invest in brushes with holes in the handles. If not, then drill through the top of the handles using the drill.

Library lamp

Materials

• Old books with red covers • Lamp with metal stem • Drill with bit to fit diameter of the stem • 45ml (1¾fl oz) paint: 2 pots red, 1 pot vermilion • Roller • Paintbrushes • Metal eyelet • MDF for making the plinth, 0.5mm

Instructions

Make the plinth according to the size of the largest book, which will form the base of the lamp. This can also be a simple box filled with wood or pebbles.

The base must be heavy enough to hold the lamp steady.

Mix the three pots of paint. Apply two coats to the plinth. Drill the plinth at the top in the centre.

Make the pile of books. Drill through the books one by one. Paint some of the covers bright red.

Dismantle the lamp, place the books onto the stem and locate the position on the plinth.

Reassemble the lamp, placing the metal eyelet in the hole of the last book. Attach the lamp holder and the shade.

Deer doily

Materials

• Lamp and little red lampshade • 2 round doilies, embroidered, in varying diameters • Red dye • Red embroidery yarn • Sewing box

Instructions

Dye the largest doily by hand or by machine. When dying, follow the manufacturer's instructions.

Embroider over the motifs on the small doily in red. Take a fine embroidery needle and go over the existing embroidery again.

Sew the small doily in the centre of the large one. Sew them onto the lampshade.

Gentleman's lampshade

Materials

• Special undercoat for wood • Matt acrylic paint (Farrow & Ball, Mahogany, no. 36)
• Recycled wooden floor lamp • Lighting fixture • 8 remnants of wool fabric
• Second-hand woollen ties • Textile glue
• Sewing kit • DIY kit

Instructions

Lightly sand the floor lamp. Apply the undercoat, then the matt acrylic paint. Assemble the lighting fixture, if necessary.

Use a real tie as a template. Transfer the template onto paper, stopping at the point where the tie would be knotted. Add 1cm (⅜in) on either side for the hems.

Cut approximately 15 to 20 ties from the remnants of wool fabric, according to the size of the shade.

Turn under 1cm (⅜in) to the inside of each tie to make the hem. Sew the hems using small invisible stitches.

Alternate real and faux ties around a suitable lampshade, overlapping them slightly.

Turn under and glue the top to the inside of the lampshade using textile glue. Sew several invisible stitches to hold the intersections of the ties in place.

Nature

In raffia

Materials

- White paint • Lamp stand • Lighting fixture
- Small toolbox

Floral lamp: • Round lampshade frame
• Raffia paper • String • Cardboard • Pins
• PVA glue • Fine paintbrush • Clothes pegs
• Double-sided sticky tape

Cork lamp: • Self-adhesive backing material
• Round lampshade frame • Cork paper
• Strips of raffia • Cutter

Instructions

For the two lamps:

Lightly sand the lampstand, then paint it white and leave to dry.

Assemble the lighting fixture. Take the measurements of the shade. The creation must adhere to the dimensions of the frame, i.e. diameter + 1cm (⅜in) by height + 2cm (¾in). If necessary, re-cut to the correct size.

Floral lamp

Make around 20 large flower shapes from string by forming loops in regular sizes and tying the centres.

Prepare the weaving for the shade. Weave strips of flat raffia. Space out the warp and weft threads to create holes. Hold the weaving in place with pins stuck into cardboard.

Secure the weaving with PVA glue to hold it in place. Paste PVA glue over the weaving using a fine paintbrush: the glue will become transparent as it dries.

Cut-out lamp

Cut a rectangle the size of the frame from the self-adhesive backing material.

Remove the protective film and stick on the cork paper. Wipe with a cloth to remove any air bubbles.

Apply a little PVA glue to the strips of raffia paper. Glue the strips vertically, spaced at regular intervals. Use the cutter to cut holes between the strips.

Lampshade assembly

Close up the cover into a ring the diameter of the lampshade. Stick together with some double-sided sticky tape.

Glue the weaving onto the lampshade frame. Apply a little PVA glue to the top and the bottom of the frame.

Turn under 1cm (⅜in) at the top and bottom of the shade, towards the inside. Hold in place with clothes pegs.

Living lamp

Materials

- Old lampstand • Lampshade frame
- Sheet of self-adhesive backing material
- Plastic foliage • Wire • DIY kit

Instructions

Cover a lampshade frame with a sheet of self-adhesive backing material. Attach a wire interlacing to it so that you can slide in branches of plastic foliage approximately 15cm (6in) in size.

You must:

- leave some space at the top.

- use a wide lampshade, so that there is space between the bulb and the leaves. The leaves must not touch the heat source.

- use a low wattage bulb.

Nature

Logs and seeds

Materials

• Silver birch log, 45cm (18in) in diameter
• Silver birch branch, 55cm (22in) in length • Requirements for the lighting fixture (electricity cable, lamp holder, elbow connector cable, plug, switch, bulb, lampshade) • Wallpaper with leaf motifs • Acorns, conkers, chestnuts, acorn cups, etc. • Drill • Linen thread • Wooden peg • Spray paper glue

Instructions

Saw the branch so that it can be fixed at an angle to the log with a wooden peg on one side. Place a lamp holder horizontally on the other side.

Cut out leaf motifs from wallpaper and glue them in a nice arrangement onto the lampshade.

Make holes in the conkers, acorns, etc. with a drill. Place the conkers in a vice when drilling to avoid hurting your fingers.

Slide the acorns, conkers, etc. onto approximately 5cm (2in) of linen thread. Finish with a knot and cut 5mm (¼in) from the knot.

Pierce a hole in the bottom of the lampshade every 3cm (1¼in) with a needle, slip the other end of the thread into the hole and tie.

Install the lighting fixture and add the lampshade.

Leafy chandelier

Materials

• Packing card • Deco paint: white, green gold and brown • Gold paint • Flat, double-ring lampshade, 40cm (16in) • Medium-sized wire • Glue gun • Components for lighting fixture • Scissors • Cutter

Instructions

Cut out six rectangles 2–3cm (¾–1¼in) wide and 42cm (16¾in) long from the packing card for the top part, 26cm (10½in) long for the bottom part of the chandelier.

Make a plain ring of wire, 10cm (4in) in diameter for the top and 5cm (2in) for the bottom. For the centre, use the lampshade ring.

Glue the longest strips of card at regular intervals between the top ring and the lampshade ring, folding under 1cm (⅜in) at each end. Intersperse the small ones, gluing them in the same way between the lampshade ring and the ring at the bottom.

Suspend the whole shade as soon as possible, so that you can work more easily, and to check that it sits evenly.

Cut out some little branches from card and glue them to the right and left of the main branches.

Cut out leaves in three different sizes. Fold them in half to mark the central vein, then glue them on to the branches.

Paint the leaves with a mixture of green gold and white, varying the proportions of the mixture. Paint the branches in brown. Highlight the branches and leaves with gold paint.

Cut out some hearts, highlight them with gold paint and glue them onto the chandelier. Paint the central ring in gold.

Assemble the lighting fixture and suspend.

Driftwood

Materials

• 6cm (2¼in) length of wood, 1.5 × 0.8cm (⅝ × ⅜in) • Piece of wood (plinth), 12 × 12cm (4¾ × 4¾in), 1.8cm (⅝in) thick • Wooden bobbin wound with thread • Hollow steel stem, 8mm (⅜in) in diameter, 45cm (18in) in length • Components for the lighting fixture • Branches of driftwood • Fine wire • Red string • Wood glue • Drill and 8mm (⅜in) bit • Red lampshade

Instructions

Cut four 1.5cm (⅝in) squares from the length of wood. Glue them beneath the plinth.

Drill a hole in the centre of the plinth. Slip the steel stem into the bobbin, then into the hole.

Pass the electricity cable inside. Assemble the lighting fixture.

Arrange the branches in a bouquet, on the bobbin and around the stem. Tie them together with fine wire, then wrap the red string around on top. Attach the lampshade.

Rustic leaves

Dimensions

Diameter: 50cm (20in)

Materials

• 5 sheets of Canson large format paper per colour: taupe, grey, brown • Self-adhesive backing material, 30 × 158cm (12 × 62¼in) • Vinyl glue
• 2 lampshade frame components, 50cm (20in)
• Clothes pegs

Instructions

Form a cylinder by sticking one end of the 30cm (12in) edges of the self-adhesive backing material onto the other.

Glue the bottom and top of the lampshade frames, on the inside, using vinyl glue (see Fig. 1). Hold in place with clothes pegs.

Cut out a sheet of Canson grey, the size of the lampshade. Remove the film from the self-adhesive backing material and glue the sheet onto the lampshade (see Fig. 2).

Enlarge and photocopy the patterns of the leaves. Cut out each leaf twice in the Canson taupe and brown paper.

Make a slit in the centre on the top half of one leaf, and on the bottom half of the other one (see Fig. 3). Fold each sheet in half along this line, then slide them into one another through the slits.

Glue onto the lampshade, varying the colours, sizes and shapes.

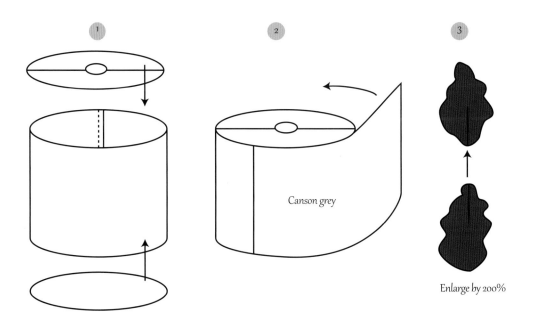

Canson grey

Enlarge by 200%

Style with string

Materials

• Wooden lampstand • Fabric lampshade
• Wood glue • Fabric glue • Assortment
of string in different widths and textures
• Elastic bands • Small hammer wrapped in a
cloth or mallet

Instructions

Lampstand: Make some plaits from string of average width, a little longer than the height of the base. Hold the ends together with a spot of glue.

Squash the plaits with the hammer then use wood glue to attach them vertically flat onto the base, fitting them snugly to the shape. Hold in place with some elastic bands while they dry, then fill the gaps between the plaits by sticking on lengths of string. Wind strips of string around on top of them.

Hold the covering of horizontal string in place in the more difficult areas, such as in the hollows.

Prepare a double length of string knotted at regular intervals, then glue it around the base.

Lampshade: Prepare three lengths of doubled string in different colours and widths, and glue them flat at the top and bottom of the lampshade, drawing a wavy line for the one just above the bottom.

Perfect pebbles

Materials

• Recycled lampstand, approximately
20cm (8in) high • Lampshade, 20cm (8in)
high • Fine string • Thick string • Flat pebbles
• Little branches of wood • Glue gun

Instructions

Surround the lampstand with little branches of wood, hiding it completely.

Attach the branches with a glue gun. Tie roughly whilst drying.

Remove the tie and, in its place, wrap the branches with thick string. Tie. Cut the string behind the knot.

Glue the pebbles flat onto the lampshade.

You can also tie the pebbles with a piece of fine string and glue them to the lampshade.

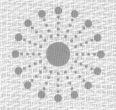

Paper

White silk

Materials

- Components for lighting fixture
- White silk paper • Wallpaper paste
- Camembert cheese box • Salad bowl
- Cling film (plastic wrap)

Instructions

Prepare the wallpaper paste one hour in advance.

Place the salad bowl upside down. Cover with cling film (plastic wrap). Place the Camembert cheese box on the salad bowl.

Soak the silk paper in the wallpaper paste. Apply to the salad bowl and the Camembert box. Leave to dry.

Remove the salad bowl and the cling film. The lampshade may still be damp beneath the cling film. Leave to dry.

Prepare the lighting fixture. Pierce the Camembert box and pass the cable inside.

Baroque lampshade

Materials

• 2 sheets of Canson paper, 70 × 102cm (28 × 40in) – 270g (9½oz) • Lampshade frame, diameter 25–30cm (10–12in), height 29cm (11½in) • Glue gun • Cutter • Pencil • Ruler

Instructions

Cut out strips of paper measuring 3 × 70cm (1¼ × 28in). Roll around the pencil up to the right side at one end for 20cm (8in) and roll in the other direction at the other end.

Place the strips at the top of the frame, folding them to different lengths. Attach them with the glue gun and alternate the strips with loops, facing towards the inside and outside. If necessary, fill the spaces with strips where only one end is rolled up.

Sheet music

Materials

• MDF, 4cm (1½in) thick • Jigsaw • Resource matt paints: grey lead, white • Undercoat • Paintbrushes • Wood screws • Wood glue • Wood filler • Components for the lighting fixture • Music scores • Double-sided sticky tape • Drill • Lampshade

Instructions

Copy or draw a treble clef. Enlarge the image on a photocopier to approximately 30cm (12in) high. Trace, then transfer to the MDF. Cut out carefully using the jigsaw.

For the plinth, cut out a circle from the MDF approximately 20cm (8in) in diameter, ensuring that it is not much larger than the bulbous part of the treble clef.

From underneath, screw/glue the plinth beneath the treble clef. Drill through the top of the treble clef and fill with wood filler. Leave to dry, then drill a hole in it to screw in the drill sleeve.

Lightly sand the cut edges and apply the undercoat. Paint grey lead matt paint onto the plinth and the outside of the treble clef and white mixed with a little of the grey on the inside of the treble clef.

Assemble the lighting fixture. Separate the sheets of music use double-sided sticky tape to attach to the lampshade, overlapping them.

Toile de Jouy print

Materials

• 3 sheets of silk paper in Toile de Jouy print or 3 sheets of Décopatch • Washi tape to match the paper • Dome lampshade frame • Beads • Double-sided sticky tape • Velvet ribbon in 2 colours, 1cm (⅜in) wide, 2m (2yd) in length

Instructions

Glue two sheets of silk paper or Décopatch together, overlapping them by 1cm (⅜in) at each end widthways to obtain a cylinder. Gather in the top, leaving an opening of 9cm (3½in) in diameter.

Cut a strip measuring 3 × 29cm (1¼ × 11½in) from the washi tape. Stick the strip of washi tape on top, overlapping the ends by 1cm (⅜in). Slip the silk paper onto the frame. Attach it at the top using double-sided sticky tape.

Puff out the silk paper all around the framework. Glue it at the bottom.

Cut strips measuring 4 × 22cm (1¾ × 8¾in) from the third sheet of paper.

Make the pompoms by folding the strip of paper in half. Cut fringes at the bottom, 3cm (1¼in) high. Roll then glue the ends.

Tie ribbons around the top. Glue the pompoms to the ends of the ribbons. Sew beads above the pompoms.

To make it sturdier, the paper can be draped around a Japanese paper ball shade.

Silk anniversary

Dimensions

20cm (8in) in diameter, 27cm (10¾in) high

Materials

• 1 plain ring and 1 ring with raised smaller ring, 20cm (8in) in diameter • Self-adhesive backing material, 27 × 63.8cm (10¾ × 25¼in) • PVC glue • Fabric paint in soft pink • Lighting fixture (bulb, lamp holder, lead, switch and plug) • White, raw silk, 30 × 63.8cm (12 x 25¼in) • Wooden clothes pegs • Pencil

Instructions

Iron the fabric to remove any creases. Glue the fabric onto the self-adhesive backing material, gradually lifting off the protective film. Smooth away the air bubbles, leaving a 1.5cm (⅝in) excess of fabric at the top and bottom. Fold and glue the excess to the reverse.

Enlarge the text, removing the coloured areas to produce a stencil. Place on the silk, 5cm (2in) from the bottom, then paint in soft pink. Leave to dry.

Close up the self-adhesive backing material into a circle, spreading glue along one edge for 1cm (⅜in) after performing a test around one of the rings. Depending on the thickness of the fabric, there may be a slight variation!

When the glue is dry, pierce a 5mm (¼in) diameter hole at the back to thread in the cable.

Glue the rings onto the inside of the lampshade, turn under and glue the excess fabric over the top with the plain ring at the top and the ring with smaller ring at the bottom, ensuring that they line up well so that the bulb is inside the lampshade.

Hold the rings in place with the clothes pegs while they dry.

Assemble the lighting fixture.

LOVE ALWAYS

CENTRE OF TEXT

5CM (2IN)

5CM (2IN) FROM THE BOTTOM OF THE LAMPSHADE

Hanging garden

Materials

• Pendant lampshade • Offcut of floral fabric with flowers, both large and small • Fusible web • Iron • Sewing box • Textile glue • Clothes pegs • Lighting fixture • Fringe

Instructions

Apply fusible web to the reverse of the floral fabric. Make 3D flowers using motifs. Cut out the large flowers several times (see Fig. 1).

You will need two identical flowers to make one large 3D flower.

Cut out one whole large flower. Cut out the petals of the second flower (see Fig. 2).

Make a slit with the scissors at the base of each petal (see Fig. 3).

Overlap the fabric to give volume and glue (see Fig. 4). If necessary, trim any fabric that overlaps (see Fig. 5).

Glue the petals onto the whole large flower. Sew several invisible stitches to make sure they are secured firmly in place (see Fig. 6).

Assemble the lighting fixture for the lampshade. Suspend it to make it easier to work with.

Use textile glue to attach a fringe to the edge. While drying, hold it in place with clothes pegs. If necessary, reinforce with several stitches using invisible thread.

Glue the flowers onto the lampshade, as if it were a climbing plant.

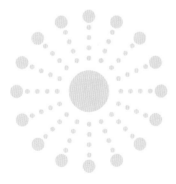

Hanging garden (cont.)

1. Carefully cut around the flowers.

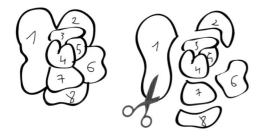

2. Use two or three identical flowers to make
a 3D one. Set aside one whole flower, which
will serve as the base. Cut out each part of the
remaining flower, following its make-up.

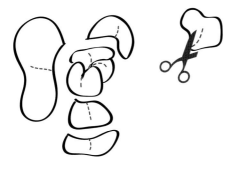

3. Make a slit using scissors at the base of each petal.

4. Overlap the fabric to give it volume. Glue.

5. If necessary, cut off any excess fabric.

6. Glue these petals to the flower base. Sew several stitches using invisible thread to make sure they are secured firmly in place.

Butterflies in bloom

Materials

- Card • White Japanese paper ball shade
- Wallpaper • Gel glue

Instructions

Cut out the butterfly silhouette in three different enlargements from card to act as a template.

Trace, then cut out lots of butterflies from the wallpaper.

Fold each butterfly in half 1mm ($^1/_{16}$in) from each side of the centre to make a flat section. Coat with gel glue, then glue onto the paper ball shade – see photo for positioning.

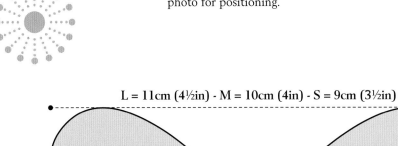

L = 11cm (4½in) - M = 10cm (4in) - S = 9cm (3½in)

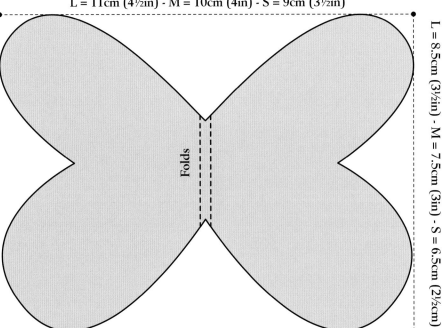

Folds

L = 8.5cm (3½in) - M = 7.5cm (3in) - S = 6.5cm (2½cm)

White light

Materials

- 4 polystyrene balls, 10cm (4in) in diameter
- White paper • UHU polystyrene glue
- Chrome-plated brass tube • Chrome-plated base cover • Connector terminal • White lamp holder • Transparent power cable with plug and switch • Lampshade frame, diameter at the top: 10cm (4in), diameter at the bottom: 35cm (14in), height: 20cm (8in) • Self-adhesive backing material, 50 × 65cm (20 × 26in)
- Tarlatan, 42 × 29.7cm (16½ × 11¾in)
- Newspaper • A4 sheet of copy paper (ribbed, embossed, with clouds, pearlised satin, onion paper) • Drill • Clothes pegs • Glue gun

Instructions

For the stand: Drill through the centre of the four balls, the size of the diameter of the brass tube.

Cut one ball in half and scoop out one of the pieces to cover the base cover.

Place the connector terminal inside the base cover and screw the chrome-plated tube on top. Slide on the hollow half-ball, which hides the base cover, then the two other balls, and finally the last one.

Tear up little pieces of paper and glue them onto the balls. Slip the transparent wire into the tube and join to the lamp holder.

For the lampshade: Copy the pattern for the lampshade using soft paper, then trace the shape onto the self-adhesive backing material. Cut out.

Cut the different A4 papers into 4 × 21cm (2¾ × 8¼in) strips. Remove the protective sheet then lay on the strips, alternating the types and overlapping them, but only sticking the parts which do not overlap.

Close up the lampshade into a circle and attach it to the frame using the glue gun. Place on the lamp holder.

Advice: N.B. the lamp holder must not be too close to the polystyrene.

Stencilled shade

Materials

- Linen lampshade • Matt acrylic paint
- Stencil brush • Stencil adhesive film
- Cutter • Cutting mat

Instructions

Create the stencil.

Using the cutter, cut out ethnic-inspired shapes in the stencil adhesive film. Remove the protective film and glue the stencil onto the lampshade.

Paint the lampshade with the stencil brush. Use the paint as it comes, without overloading the paintbrush and by tapping on the motifs to cover them with paint. Vary the degree of pressure to create different effects.

Leave to dry, then move the stencil, checking that it is always well positioned, both horizontally and vertically.

You could reproduce the same stencil on the wall.

Floral silhouette

Materials

• Sheet of Cromático tracing paper, 200g (7oz), colour Spring and Yellow, 50 × 65cm (20 × 26in) Thibierge & Comar • Lid of a Camembert cheese box • Double-sided sticky tape • Neoprene glue • Tube of paint for wood, colour mandarin • Plastic wire housing: plastic cylinder that screws onto an electricity cable and holds the pendant light fitting in place • Wooden pencil and eraser • Set square • Protractor • Extending compasses (or traditional compasses, string and drawing pin) • Scissors • Electrician's screwdriver • Precision cutter • 2mm (¹⁄8in) hole punch • Drill with 5mm (¼in) drill bit • Paintbrush

Instructions

The pendant is made up of two overlaying tracing paper lampshades.

Calculation of the dimensions:

The dimensions can be adapted as you wish; only the diameter of the top ring of the lampshade is dependent upon the diameter of the lid of the Camembert box.

Transfer the green diagram from the pattern onto green tracing paper, bearing in mind your specific dimensions. Trace onto two perpendicular drawing lines:

AB = radius of large ring of the lampshade; AC = height of the lampshade; CD = radius of small ring of the lampshade.

Trace a straight line passing through B and D; you will find O – the centre of the curves passing through A and C.

Calculate the angle of the opening: $\{(AB - CD) \times 360\}/AC$. Transfer this angle onto O.

Green tracing paper:

Cut out the pattern that you have just traced. Erase the drawing lines.

Trace a 1cm (⅜in) gap freehand all around the pattern.

Draw some flowers, stems and umbelliferae leaves.

Remove all the gaps between the flowers and the foliage by using the precision cutter (make sure you retain the margins around the edge). Perforate all the flowers with the 2mm (¹⁄8in) hole punch.

Yellow tracing paper:

Make the second lampshade in yellow tracing paper by transferring the pattern from the green tracing paper with the same dimensions.

Add a turn-back for closing up the lampshade and trace a third curve starting at O, but cutting the straight line AC 1cm (⅜in) above point C (see the yellow areas on the pattern).

Paper

Floral silhouette (cont.)

Pierce a 5mm (¼in) hole in the centre of the Camembert box, then paint it in mandarin. Leave to dry.

Dismantle the lamp holder from the cable of the ceiling light, slide on the wire housing and then the box.

Reassemble the lamp holder. Screw together the wire housing to hold the box. Screw in a 25 watt max. bulb.

Finishes: Lightly apply some glue to the top part of the green lampshade and the edge of the Camembert box.

Leave to dry a little, then place the lampshade onto the edge of the box. Place a length of sticky tape on the turn-back of the yellow lampshade and wrap it over itself around the green lampshade. Press down firmly.

Advice: To trace a curve without a pair of compasses, insert a drawing pin at one end of a piece of string at the start of the curve and wrap it around a pencil at the other end. Stretch the string when tracing and turning.

N.B. you will need to take several precautions (turn off the electricity supply, check the assembly, etc.).

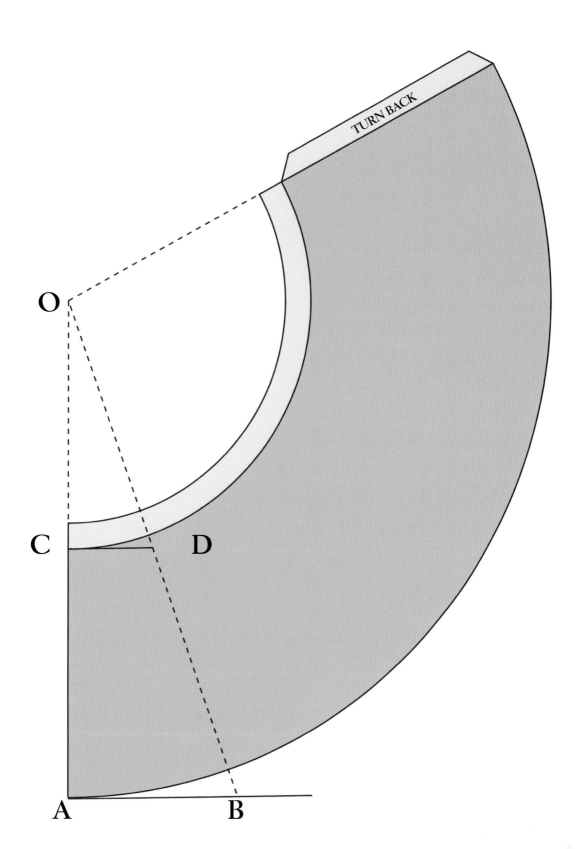

TURN BACK

O

C   D

A   B

Memories

Photo booth

Materials

• Lamp with 15cm (6in) lampshade
• 10 small bulldog clips • 10 black and white passport-sized photos with different pictures

Instructions

Clip rows of four passport-sized photos showing different pictures on top of the lampshade using bulldog clips.

Advice: make little themed lampshades: fancy dress, children, holidays, etc. You can also print your photos in black and white on cardboard and cut the strips using a cutter.

Happy holidays

Materials

• Plain lampshade ring, 50cm (20in) in diameter • Flat lampshade ring with smaller ring, 50cm (20in) in diameter • Self-adhesive backing material, 30 × 162cm (24 × 46½in) • Fairly thick linen panel, 30 × 168cm (12 × 65in) • White organza cotton, 50cm (20in) • PVC glue • Clothes pegs • Gouache or watercolours • Several images (plain on the reverse); displayed here: map, old postcards, etc.

Instructions

Prepare the items for the windows. The old postcard has been retouched using heavily diluted gouache, then printed as a transfer onto the white organza.

Cut out a piece of map to the desired size.

Arrange the items on the reverse of the linen panel, centre them and space out evenly along the length of the linen.

Mark the outlines, then draw a frame on the reverse of the linen, 5mm (¼in) from the edges.

Cut each window, allowing for a turn-back of 1cm (⅜in) all the way around and for a neat edge. Make small cuts at each corner. Iron the turn-back towards the reverse.

Then line up each image in its position on the reverse of the linen and stick the self-adhesive backing material on top. Wipe a cloth from the centre towards the outside of each image to remove any air bubbles.

Once the strip is finished, make a double turn-back of 1.5cm (⅝in) at each end and attach it using PVC glue.

Line up the double ring at the top and the plain ring at the bottom using clothes pegs. Close up the ring by sticking the two ends to each other.

Turn under the fabric over the rings at the top and bottom, making a double turn-back. Glue and hold in place with clothes pegs or by pressing together firmly (fast drying).

Memories

Hit the road

Materials

- White lampshade • Old road map
- Spray glue • Braid • Cutter • Scissors
- PVA glue • Paintbrush

Instructions

Apply glue to the whole lampshade. Use spray glue for an even distribution. Glue the road map onto the shade and leave to dry.

Fold down the map at the top and bottom to fit the size of the lampshade.

Where the map overlaps around the shade, carefully cut through the upper layer to create a neat edge at the join.

Glue braid to the top and bottom using PVA glue.

Memories

Private showing

Materials

- Square-shaped lampshade frame • 120 slides
- Pair of cutting pliers • Reel of fine wire
- Fine spiral drill

Instructions

Drill holes with the spiral drill into the four sides of each slide, right in the centre of each side.

Cut up some little pieces of wire. Bend them into rings and thread them through the holes in the slides, attaching them to each other at the four sides. You will need approximately 30 slides to cover one side of the shade.

Then attach the strips of slides to the top and bottom of the shade, so that they go completely around it.

Advice: you can also glue the slides directly onto a white lampshade, using PVA glue or vinyl glue. Apply the glue to the plastic or card part of the slides.

Memories

Trinket shade

Materials

• Recycled lamp with lampshade
• Collection of flat lucky charms for sewing on or gluing (pendants, medals, coins, keys, etc.)
• Strong glue • Large rocaille beads • Small rocaille beads • Sewing box

Instructions

Sand and repaint the lampstand if needed. Sew on all the little lucky charms or attach using strong glue. Intersperse all sorts of little mementos. The more personal your items, the more original your lampshade will be.

Sew little beaded hanging items from the top and bottom of the shade: slide on small and large rocaille beads alternately.

When you get to the last bead, thread the wire back into the last-but-one bead and bring it back out at the base of the lampshade.

Continue all around the shade. Add some hanging medals too.

Step-by-step guides

Using knitting for your décor

General points

The band or label on each ball of yarn holds some useful information, i.e. the composition of the yarn, number of recommended needles, number of stitches and rows for a sample swatch, 10cm (4in) knitted in stocking stitch (knit 1 row, purl 1 row) (see Fig. 1) and care instructions.

Sample swatch

You must knit a sample swatch using the intended stitch and the recommended needles.

To be sure that you have a 10cm (4in) sample swatch, cast (bind) on more stitches than are stated on the ball of yarn. So, knit approximately 15cm (6in) in the stitch of the item you are going to make and loosely cast (bind) off. Spread out the sample, without pulling it. Place a ruler horizontally in the centre. Position two pins 10cm (4in) apart (see Fig. 2).

Count the number of stitches between the pins. For the items suggested here, the number of rows is less important, as the lengths will be checked by placing the slightly stretched knitting against the objects.

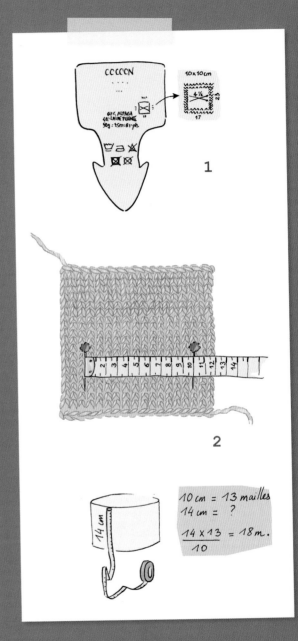

GAUGE FOR CHECKING THE
DIAMETER OF NEEDLES

Number of stitches to cast on

Measure the object to be covered, then do a simple multiplication and division calculation based on the number of stitches in the sample swatch.

You will need

- Balls of yarn ● Knitting needles
- 1m (1yd) of ribbon ● Ruler
- Long flat-headed pins
- Darning needle ● Scissors ● Gauge

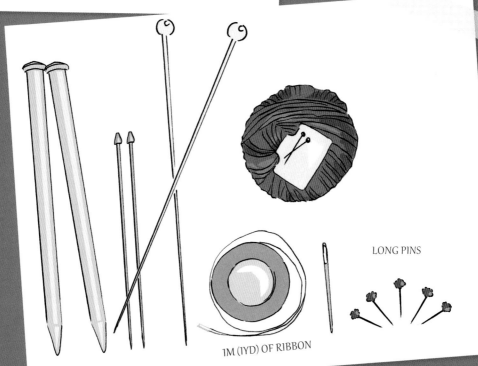

1M (1YD) OF RIBBON

LONG PINS

Scoobies

The scoobies used in the projects are in two thicknesses: fine and wide. The 90cm (35½in) long ones are long enough for all the items, apart from the wide strands of the pink lampshade, which are sold in 2m (2yd) lengths.

Mastering the knots and spacing requires practice. It is best to practise with flat items using string or scoobies, before starting on the lampshades.

Experience of macramé would be useful!

All the items use the same techniques: starting knots, flat knots, baguette knots (see diagrams).

To finish the work, simply tie the strands by pulling them. Their elasticity will hold them in place.

The frames of all the shades are painted the same colour as the scoobies, then, after drying, they are completely wrapped with strands to hide them.

The strands that are not used for weaving have therefore been used for covering the frames.

Starting knot: fold each strand in half. Place the loop in front of the wire of the frame. Fold it back and pull the two ends through the loop. Pull tight.

Flat knot: this is generally made with four strands: the two outside strands work around the two central strands (guide).

Stretch the guide taut, pass the left strand to the right, under the guide and over the right strand (1).

Pass the right strand over the guide and into the loop formed by the left strand (2). Pull tight regularly.

Take the right strand and pass it towards the left under the guide and over the left strand. Pass the left strand towards the right, over the guide and into the loop of the right strand (3). Pull the strands tight to secure the knot and continue in this way making knots.

Baguette knot: you can use it either to cover another strand when making diamonds, for example, or to attach one end of the strand to its support, keeping a maximum length in work (see diagram).

Diagonal baguettes: (see diagrams).

Diamonds: for each diamond, use 24 strands. Each stitch starts with a flat knot on the four centre strands. Starting with this knot, the two right strands serve as a guide for the right side and the two left strands as a guide for the left side. There are then 20 strands available for the central motif. Make a baguette knot with each of the 20 strands around each of the two guide strands placed on the bias (the diagram shows a single guide strand). At mid-height, tighten the 20 centre strands again: take the two right strands and, passing them over the top, make a flat loop right at the left edge of the centre strands and take the strands back to the right (you have four strands waiting on the horizontal on the right side, inside the diamond). Take the two left strands and, passing underneath the centre strands, wrap around the strands waiting on the right. Take the left strands back towards the left and pull on the right and left ones at the same time to tighten the centre. Start the diamond again by reversing the direction of the work. Finish with a flat knot.

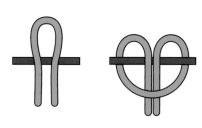

CASTING ON WARP STRANDS

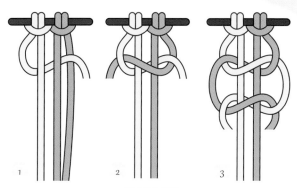

FLAT KNOTS

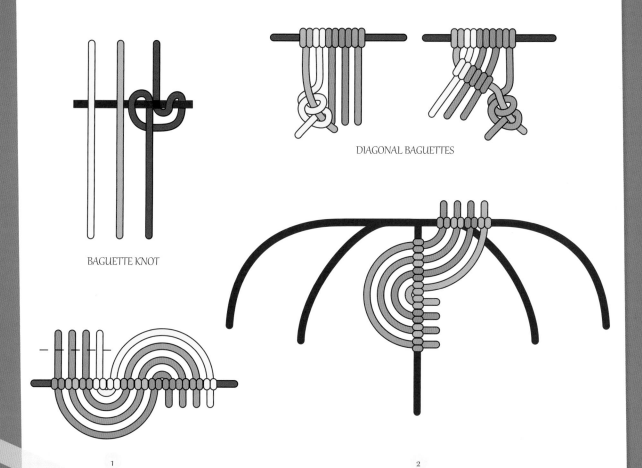

BAGUETTE KNOT

DIAGONAL BAGUETTES

List of suppliers

Lampshade frames
www.needcraft.co.uk
www.follyandglee.bigcartel.com
www.homecrafts.co.uk
www.web-crafts.co.uk

Electrical equipment, lampshade bases
www.homebase.co.uk
www.ikea.com
www.wickes.co.uk
www.johnlewis.com

General craft supplies
www.stitchcraftcreate.co.uk
www.hobbycraft.co.uk
www.fredaldous.co.uk

Wool
www.dmccreative.co.uk
www.blacksheepwools.com
www.deramores.com
www.worldofwool.co.uk

Haberdashery
www.thevillagehaberdashery.co.uk
www.guthrie-ghani.co.uk
www.abakhan.co.uk
www.simplysewing.co.uk

Paper
www.decopatch.com
www.designersguild.com
www.farrow-ball.com
www.paper.co.uk

Self adhesive material
www.art2screen.co.uk
www.fredaldous.co.uk
www.needcraft.co.uk
www.martin-dannell.co.uk

Fabric
www.brunschwig.com
www.dylon.co.uk
www.frumble.co.uk
www.stitchcraftcreate.co.uk

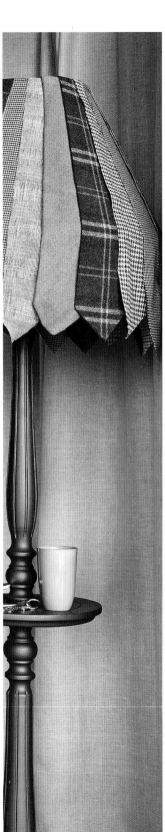

A DAVID & CHARLES BOOK
© Éditions Marie Claire – Société d'Information et de Créations - SIC, 2013

Originally published in French as Abat-jour

First published in the UK and USA in 2013 by F&W Media International, Ltd
David & Charles is an imprint of F&W Media International, Ltd
Brunel House, Forde Close, Newton Abbot, TQ12 4PU, UK

F&W Media International, Ltd is a subsidiary of F+W Media, Inc 10151
Carver Road, Suite #200, Blue Ash, OH 45242, USA

Names of manufacturers and product ranges are provided for the information
of readers, with no intention to infringe copyright or trademarks.

A catalogue record for this book is available from the British Library.

ISBN-13: 978-1-4463-0445-7 paperback
ISBN-10:1-4463-0445-0 paperback

Printed in China by RR Donnelley for:
F&W Media International, Ltd
Brunel House, Forde Close, Newton Abbot, TQ12 4PU, UK

10 9 8 7 6 5 4 3 2 1

Publisher: Thierry Lamarre
Head of publishing: Adeline Lobut
Proofreading/editing: Isabelle Misery
Technical specifications: Intérieur Lumière
Technical proofing: Clémentine Lubin
Image search: Sylvie Creusy
Graphic design and layout: Either studio
Cover: Either studio

F+W Media publishes high quality books on a wide range of subjects.

For more great book ideas visit: www.stitchcraftcreate.co.uk